MAKE it WORK!
PLANTS

Wendy Baker & Andrew Haslam

written by
Claire Watts and Alexandra Parsons

Photography: Jon Barnes
Series Consultant: John Chaldecott
Science Consultant: Bob Press
Professional Botanist

TWO-CAN

MAKE it WORK!
Other Titles

Earth
Electricity
Sound

First published in Great Britain in 1992 by
Two-Can Publishing Ltd
346 Old Street,
London EC1V 9NQ
in association with Scholastic Publications Ltd

Copyright © Two-Can Publishing Ltd, 1992
Design © Wendy Baker and Andrew Haslam, 1992

Printed in Hong Kong

2 4 6 8 10 9 7 5 3

British Library Cataloguing in Publication Data
          Baker, Wendy
          Plants – (Make it work!)
          I. Title II. Haslam, Andrew III. Series
          581.07

          ISBN: 1-85434-129-4

Editors: Claire Watts and Mike Hirst
Illustrator: Diana Leadbetter
Children's photography: Matthew Ward

Additional thanks to: Albert Baker, Catherine Bee, Tony Ellis, Elaine
Gardner, Nick Hawkins, Claudia Sebire and everyone at Plough Studios

Contents

Words marked in **bold** are explained in the glossary.

Scientists study the world around them and the way it works. They investigate a huge variety of subjects, from electricity to the behaviour of humans and animals. Learning about plant life is known as botany – a branch of biology, the study of all living things. Botanists find out about the structure of plants, their natural functions, **environments** and uses.

MAKE it WORK!

In this book you will explore the science of botany. As you follow the projects in the book, you will be investigating the plant world for yourself. It is very important to use scientific methods. Draw pictures of different stages of your investigation as accurately as you can, or take photos. Make sure you label all your specimens so you can identify them later.

Scientists use thorough, step-by-step methods to study their subjects. They observe carefully and then record their observations accurately. They use their observations to form **theories** and then do experiments to test these theories. It may take many experiments before any definite answers are found.

▲ Use tweezers to handle delicate flowers, leaves and seeds. Keep your specimens sealed in plastic bags until you need them.

▶ Keep careful records and file them away so that you can refer to them easily.

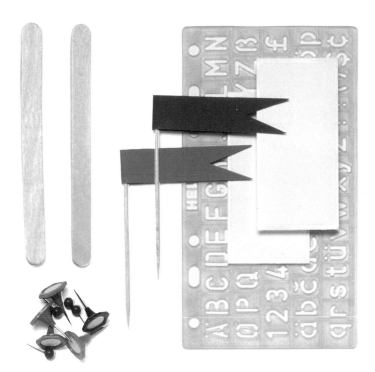

Cardboard Make a collection of thick and thin cardboard from boxes and cartons. You should find it useful for lots of different projects.

Coloured card It is useful to have different colours of card, but if you do not have any you could paint plain card with poster paints.

Paper Look out for paper of different thicknesses and textures. Keep a big pile of rough paper for practising on. Reuse paper whenever you can.

Ruler Use a ruler for making accurate measurements. A protractor and set square may be helpful too.

▲ Always label things clearly so you can tell what they are.

You will need
All the equipment needed to do these projects is easily available. You should be able to find most of the things you need around the house or in a craft shop.

Glue Use an all-purpose glue unless you are told otherwise. If you need a waterproof glue, rubber solution glue is best.

Scissors Take care when using scissors. Blunt-ended ones are the safest type to use.

Craft knife A sharp craft knife is useful for cutting accurately, but be very careful when you use one. Ask an adult to help you.

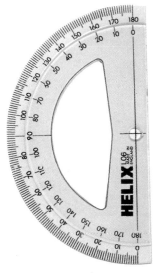

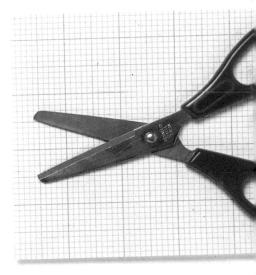

Collections of **specimens** are very important to scientists. By collecting, **cataloguing** and comparing samples of plant life, botanists try to discover differences and similarities between **species** of plants. The collection and study of such **data** is vital to all science.

MAKE it WORK!

Make your own collection of different kinds of plant specimens. Then make a box to store and display it.

You will need

thick card	glue or tape
a ruler	cocktail sticks
a pencil	lollipop sticks
craft knife	coloured paper

1 Work out what size you want your box. Cut out a flat shape like the one in the photograph on the right.

2 Draw lines on your box to mark the exact position of the dividers.

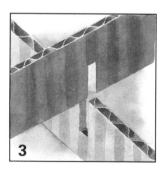

3 Make the dividers by cutting strips the same height as the box. Slot them together by cutting a slit half way up one divider and half way down the other.

4 Fold up the sides of the box. Tuck in the corner flaps and glue or tape them in place. Push the dividers into place in the box.

tissue paper

cotton wool

sawdust

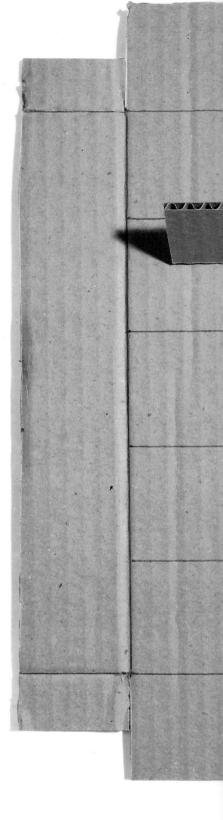

5 Give the box a bed of sawdust, cotton wool or tissue paper before you add your collection of specimens.

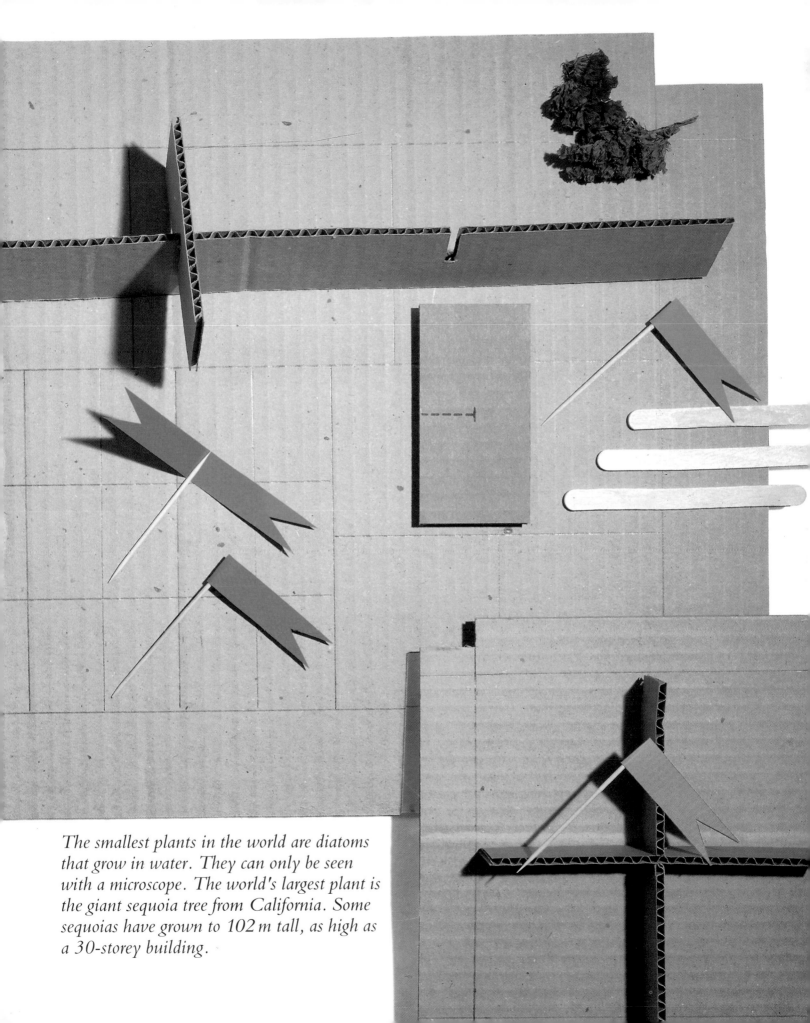

The smallest plants in the world are diatoms that grow in water. They can only be seen with a microscope. The world's largest plant is the giant sequoia tree from California. Some sequoias have grown to 102 m tall, as high as a 30-storey building.

Plants were the first forms of life on Earth. Non-flowering plants appeared more than 570 million years ago. Early dinosaurs fed on giant ferns and gingko trees. Later, flowering plants such as the magnolia developed.

No one knows exactly how many species of plant there are in the world. There may be over 240,000 species of flowering plant alone. Other major plant groups are **ferns**, **conifers**, **lichens**, **mosses**, **algae** and **fungi**.

Labelling

Sort your specimens into different categories such as seeds, flowers and nuts. Try to find out the names of your specimens by using books or asking other people. Make clear labels from ice lolly sticks or make flags from coloured paper and cocktail sticks. These will help you identify your specimens easily in the future. Attach these labels to the different sections of the box with tape or glue. Try to find out the scientific names for your specimens and write these on the labels too.

In 1753, a scientist called Linnaeus invented a system of Latin names to classify the natural world. Plants are given a two-part name. The first part refers to the genus (or family) that the plant belongs to. The second part is the name of the species within that family. For example, the silver birch tree is called Betula Pendula. Betula is the birch tree and Pendula is the species name.

▼ Try making a double layer in one part of the box. Cut the dividers half the height of the box. Then use the same method as before to build a small, shallow tray to fit on top.

All living things grow if they are given food, and plants are no exception. In fact, unlike humans and animals, plants keep on growing all their lives. They make their food from minerals and salts in the soil, from sunlight and from the gas **carbon dioxide** which is found in air and water.

MAKE it WORK!

All plants and trees have to start somewhere. Huge oak trees were once acorns and a field of ripe corn was once a sackful of seed. All it took to make them grow were sunshine, rain and fertile soil. Experiment with three different ways to grow plants: from seed, from a bulb and from a cutting. You can buy seeds and bulbs from a gardening shop. To make a cutting, you should cut a stalk off a healthy plant, just where it joins the main stem.

cress seeds

sweetcorn

broad beans

▲ Seeds come in all kinds of shape and size.

You will need

a shallow dish
cress seeds
potting compost
a cutting from an existing plant
two flower pots and saucers
a glass of water

blotting paper
small stones
a bulb

1 Sow the cress seeds Cut a circle of blotting paper to fit the bottom of the shallow dish. Moisten it with water and sprinkle on the cress seeds. Keep the blotting paper moist and just watch the cress sprout. When it gets tall enough, harvest your crop with scissors and sprinkle it on salads or in egg sandwiches.

▲ After two days the cress seeds will have swelled up and sent out curly shoots.

▲ After four days, little green leaves will have appeared. Within six days your cress will be ready to eat.

daffodil bulb

hyacinth bulbs

2 Plant the bulb Put a layer of small stones in the saucer of your plant pot – this is to help the water drain out of the pot so the bulb doesn't get waterlogged and soggy.

Fill the plant pot with potting compost, and bury the bulb in the centre. The pointed end of the bulb should be about 1cm below the surface of the compost.

Keep the compost moist and put the pot in a dark cupboard until a green shoot breaks through. Then bring it out into the light. Bulbs should be watered little and often.

Air is a mixture of oxygen, carbon dioxide and other gases. Each life form needs some of these gases to live. Humans take in oxygen and breathe out carbon dioxide. Plants take in carbon dioxide and give out oxygen.

3 Root the cutting Put the stem of the cutting into a glass of water. Check every day to see if roots are beginning to develop. Then plant it in potting compost. Water regularly.

12 Measuring Growth

Not all plants grow at the same rate. Some plants have a life cycle of only one year; corn for instance, which is sown after the winter frosts, starts to grow in spring, ripens in summer and is ready for harvesting in the autumn. Other plants, particularly trees, take years to mature and keep on growing for centuries.

Most green plants grow in just two ways. They shoot up from the tips of their stems and down from the tips of their roots. Woody plants such as trees and shrubs grow up and down too, but they also spread outwards. Every year they add a layer to their trunks, making them fatter.

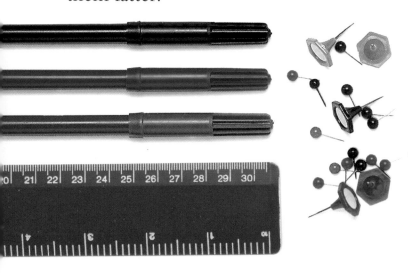

MAKE it WORK!

Plants grow because, like humans, they have growth **hormones**. These hormones control the way a plant grows, making sure that roots go down and stems go up. This up and down growth is called primary growth. Increase in width is known as secondary growth. Measure the primary growth of a house plant and a cress seed. Then measure the leaves too to see how they spread as they grow.

You will need

a ruler	card
wooden sticks	drawing pins
glue	paint

Measuring root and stem growth

1 Make a measuring stick out of card. Using the ruler, mark it out in millimetres, putting zero in the centre and running the measurements out to both ends. The pointed end is going to be the root end.

2 Plant a batch of cress, and take one seedling out each day to measure it. Place the seed on the zero and keep a record of the root growth towards one end of the measuring stick and the stem growth towards the other.

day 1

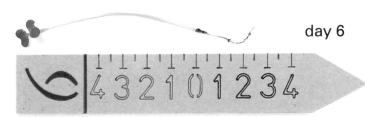

day 4

day 6

Many trees have a fairly short annual growing season, in the spring and summer. If a tree is cut down, you can see rings in the trunk, made by the different layers of growth each year. By counting the rings, you can tell how old the tree is.

Measuring stem growth

Take a young, healthy houseplant and into its pot put a tall, wooden stick. Make labels out of card and glue them onto the stick to mark the plant's progress. You could measure every week or every month, depending on how quickly the plant grows.

Try measuring different types of plant. Do some grow more quickly than others?

Measuring leaf growth

1 This is a project for the spring time, when new leaves start their life cycle. Draw out a measuring card like the one above.

2 At regular intervals, take a leaf from the same tree. Using a paint brush, cover the leaf with thick paint.

3 Make a print of your leaf. (This is explained in more detail on page 28.) When the paint has dried, cut around the leaf shape.

4 Glue your leaf print onto the measuring card.

Most plants draw up water from the ground through their roots. Water travels up the stem of the plant into the leaves and flowers. Some of the water is used by the plant to make food, and some of it **evaporates** into the air through the surface of the leaves.

MAKE it WORK!

Here's a way to watch how water travels up the stems of plants. Try the experiment with different types of white flower to see which work best. You could try a stick of celery too.

You will need

white flowers	food colouring
glass containers	cardboard
water	tape

1 Fill several glass containers with water and add different food colourings to each one. You will probably have to use quite a lot of food colouring to make the water dark enough for this experiment to work.

2 Place a flower in each vase and leave it while the stem sucks up the coloured water.

3 Watch the flowers turn different colours as the water travels up the stem to reach them. It may take several hours or even a day.

▼ Make a multi-coloured flower! Split the stalk of one flower in two up the middle. Fill two glass containers with different colours. Then place one half of the stalk in one vase and one half in the other.

Botanists have discovered that a single Winter rye plant can grow over 622 km of roots in less than one tenth of a cubic metre.

Keeping a Record

Make a **calibrated** measuring stick out of card so you can check the amount of water a plant uses. Keep a record of how much water is lost over a period of time. Compare various flowers and plants: you will find that some are thirstier than others.

▲ A cactus has very shallow, wide-spreading roots to catch the rare desert rain. It also absorbs mist and dew through its spines.

Plants have adapted to different climates in different parts of the world. Some places are hot and dry, others cold and wet, but almost every part of the world sustains some plant life.

MAKE it WORK!

Bulrushes grow in wet marshes and mugla trees grow in the hot, dry Australian desert. Pine trees grow in snow-bound forests and seaweed grows in the sea. Think of plants that grow in different environments and use them to play the environment game shown over the page.

You will need

coloured card	glue
a craft knife	a pencil
squared paper	a ruler
cardboard	

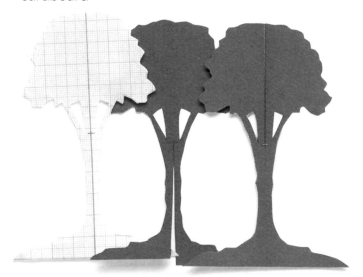

1 First make the plants. Choose four different environments and decide on a type of plant to use as a symbol for each environment. Trace the plant's shape twice onto coloured card and cut out the two shapes. Make slits in the cut-outs and slot them together so that the plant will stand up. You should make four of each plant symbol. Use different coloured card for each type of plant.

2 Make the board. Rule a piece of card with twelve lines across and twelve lines down. Then cut some small squares out of coloured card – thirteen each of red, yellow and blue, and five of black. Lay them out to make a path around the board like the one below. At each corner stick on a starting arrow.

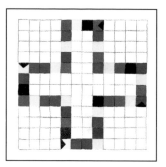 

3 Now make the four big environment corners for the board – one for each type of plant, in the matching colour. Divide each corner into four big squares and sixteen smaller ones.

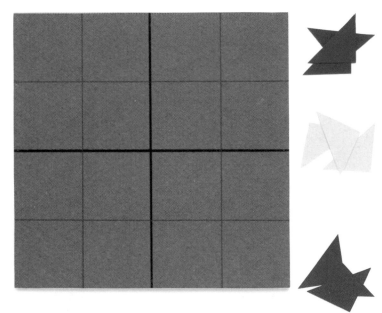

4 Make climate triangles – red represents heat, blue is water and yellow is light. Glue these climate triangles onto the environment corners, to make the right environments for your plants. For instance, a desert should have mainly red and yellow triangles, a marshy riverside mainly blue and yellow ones.

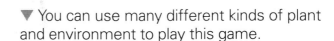
You can use many different kinds of plant and environment to play this game.

Australian desert   marsh

5 Make the playing pieces. Each player needs three pyramids made from the same colour card as their plants. Cut a triangle out of graph paper, making the base the same length as one of the squares on the board. Draw around the triangle five times, each time placing the long edges side by side. Then fold and glue the pyramid together as shown.

6 Make climate pyramids to match your climate triangles. You need twelve of red, blue and yellow. In the game, you have to collect the right colour of climate pyramids needed to grow plants in your environment corner.

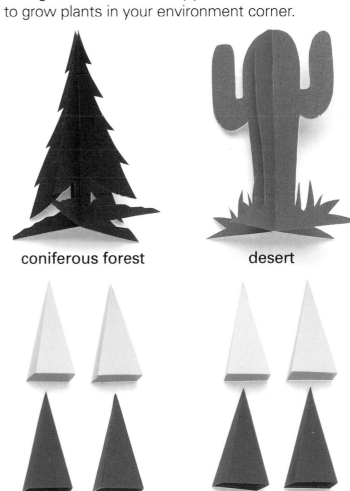

rainforest   sea   coniferous forest   desert

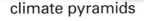

climate pyramids

Environment Game

The aim is to collect enough heat, light and water to grow plants in your environment corner. But take care! If you land on a black square, you suffer an ecological disaster.

1 Players start the game with their three playing pieces on the starting arrow in their corner of the board. The blue, yellow and red climate pyramids are stacked in the middle.

2 Take it in turns to throw the die. Players move their pieces clockwise, and may move any one of their three pieces.

3 When you land on a coloured square, pick up a pyramid of that colour and put it on one of your matching climate squares. When the four climate squares that make up a section are covered, put the pyramids back in the centre and take a plant. Hooray!

4 If you can't avoid landing on a black square, your environment suffers an ecological disaster. You lose all your pyramids, but any plants may remain.

5 If you land on the same square as another player's piece, you may take a pyramid from that player's environment.

6 The winner is the first player to plant all four plants in her or his environment corner.

Most plants change with the seasons. When there is plenty of sun and rain they grow fast, putting out new shoots and leaves. In cold or dry seasons they often appear to stop growing altogether. **Deciduous** trees have broad, flat leaves that give off a lot of moisture. They drop their leaves in autumn in order to conserve water and energy during the freezing winter months.

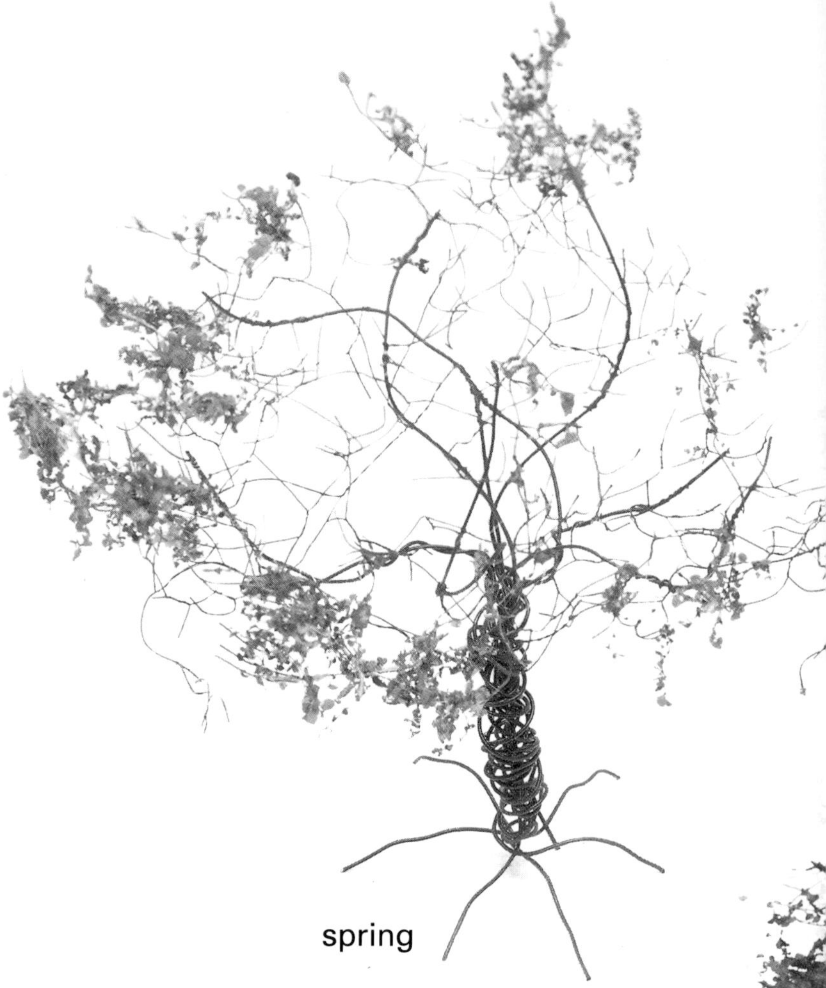

spring

winter

You will need
wire – three different thicknesses
wire cutters
pliers
moss or foam rubber
enamel modelling paint
rubber solution glue

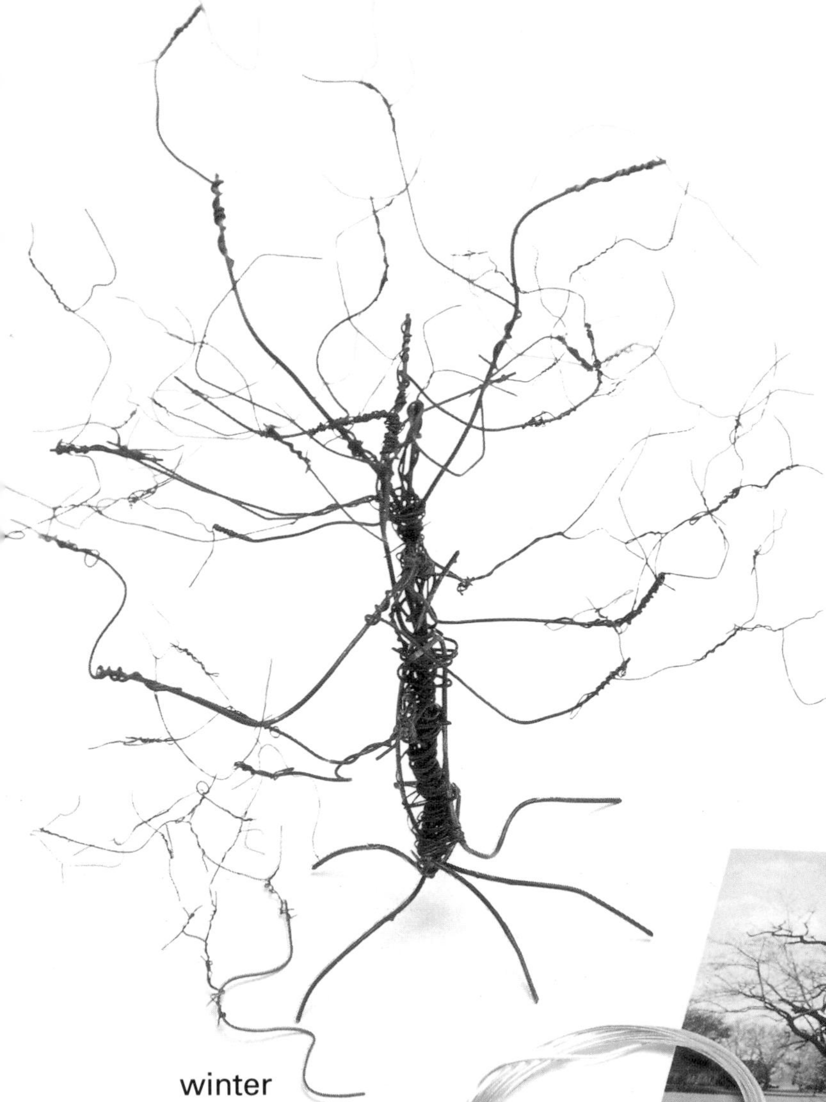

MAKE it WORK!

These tree sculptures show how trees change with the seasons. Base your models on a real tree if you can. You could take photos of a tree to help you. Look carefully at the way the branches gradually get narrower and divide.

1 Start by winding several thick pieces of wire together to form the trunk and main branches. You may have to use pliers to bend the wire. Take care because wire can be sharp.

2 Attach a number of branches made of medium wire to each main branch. To the branches attach twigs made from thin wire.

autumn

summer

◀ Ask an adult to help you cut the wire into short lengths to make your trees.

3 Make three more trees in the same way. Paint the winter and autumn trees dark. Paint the spring and summer twigs green.

4 Look around for tiny-leafed mosses or creeping plants to use for the leaves. If you cannot find any, use little pieces of foam rubber. It will not look quite the same as using real leaves, but this is a work of art, after all.

5 Stick a few leaves onto the spring tree and dab them with light green paint. Stick plenty of leaves onto the summer tree and dab them with dark green paint. Dab the autumn leaves with red or orange and scatter a few around the base of the tree, as if they had fallen off.

Not everywhere in the world has four seasons. In the tropics, close to the Equator, it is hot all year round. There are just two seasons: the dry season and the wet one.

The biggest of all plants are trees. They have thick, woody stems which divide into branches. If you look carefully at the way the branches of a tree grow, you will start to notice a pattern. Each species of tree has a distinctive shape.

MAKE it WORK!

Look at the shapes of the trees around you. Some trees are tall and narrow, others have a wide, round shape. Although most of them have green leaves, there is a lot of variety in the shades of green. Find out about unusual trees by looking in books and magazines. Which trees grow together? Which ones stand alone? Try making your own cardboard forest.

You will need

squared paper	a pencil
tracing paper	card
large sheets of paper	a craft knife
large pieces of card	a long ruler

oak

1 Draw the outline of a tree on paper. You may need to practise on rough paper first to make your tree shape really accurate.

2 Trace your drawing onto card and cut it out with a craft knife. Trace it again and cut out an identical tree.

The world needs trees because, like all plants, they use up carbon dioxide and give out oxygen. Trees help to protect the balance of gases in the Earth's atmosphere.

Lombardy poplar   North American ash

3 Cut a slit from the top of one tree shape to the middle, and from the bottom of the other to the middle. Slot them together.

4 Find out what other kinds of tree grow near your tree, and make some more models. Place them all together to make a model forest.

▼ You can use the same technique to make giant trees. Draw big squares on a large sheet of paper. Copy the lines from each square of your original drawing into the big squares. Transfer the outline onto large pieces of card cut from boxes, and slot together as before.

The trunk of a tree is a complex system of cells: storage cells; strong supporting cells; and **sap** cells that carry water and nutrients to every part of the tree. The trunk is protected by the bark that surrounds it. Bark is made up of dead cells. It varies in texture and thickness from tree to tree. Some barks are thick and deeply ridged, others are thin and smooth. As a tree grows, the bark splits and forms cracks where mosses grow and beetles and spiders find shelter.

MAKE it WORK!

In order to compare and contrast the different textures and appearances of bark, do a series of bark rubbings, file them and label them with the type of tree and the date on which the rubbings were made.

You will need

coloured paper
wax crayons
ring clips
sticky tape
hole punch
thick card

1 When you go outside to do your bark rubbing, take with you some sheets of coloured paper (A4 size is best), sticky tape and some wax crayons.

2 Inspect the trunk of the tree to find an interesting area of bark and stick your paper over it. Masking tape is the best kind of tape to use as it will stick to bark, and you will be able to peel it off later without ruining your paper.

3 Now rub the paper with a wax crayon and the pattern of the bark should emerge. Rub gently, building up the colour gradually, otherwise the paper may tear.

4 Once back from your field trip, it is time to file and catalogue your findings. Make a folder using two pieces of stiff card and two ring clips. Your file can be half A4 size, or even smaller, as you are going to cut out the best bit from your rubbing to go on file.

5 Now label the rubbings, date them, punch holes in the top and file them. You can also take rubbings of the leaves and catalogue them in the same way.

Tree bark is useful stuff. A substance called tannin is extracted from the bark of the pine tree, for instance. It is used to turn animal skins into leather. The bark of the willow gives us aspirin which is used in medicines, and the bark of the cork oak gives us bottle stoppers and cork tiles.

Leaves make food for the plant. The ingredients they need are: water, which is sucked up from the roots; carbon dioxide which is one of the gases found in air; and sunlight. This process is called **photosynthesis**. The result is a kind of sugary starch which is fed to all parts of the plant as sap. Photosynthesis takes place in the spongy layer of cells inside the leaf. The protective surface of the leaf lets in air, while water and sap flow through its veins.

MAKE it WORK!

Some leaves are a pale golden green, others a dark coppery red. Some leaves are soft and thick, others hard and shiny. Just take the time to look! Make some leaf sculptures using as many different kinds of leaves as you can find. Here are a few ideas to get you going. You could photograph the results or watch them dry and change colour.

Leaves are a vital part of every plant, and because each species of plant has a different environment and a different set of needs, leaves are as varied as the plants or trees they come from. The green in leaves comes from **chlorophyll***, a chemical in leaf cells that is necessary for the food-making process.*

▼ **Leaf box** Cut out a cube of flower-arranging foam and, using 'pins' made from sharpened twigs, pin big leaves all around it. Or you could cut out a ball of foam and cover it with circular leaves such as nasturtium leaves.

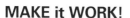

◀ Leaf forest Take a selection of leaves that are different colours. Slip each leaf into the split end of a cocktail stick. Poke the sticks into a sheet of paper and secure them underneath with sticky tape.

▶ Leaf hanging Use a big needle and some button twist or fishing line to thread a collection of leaves together. Hang them from a shelf or from the ceiling and watch the colours change.

▼ Fern of ferns This fern shape has been made from different sizes of fern leaf. You could make a giant oak-leaf shape out of oak leaves or an ivy-leaf shape from ivy leaves.

Ferns usually grow in damp, shady places. They are amongst the oldest types of plant found on Earth, and, although they have no flowers, have a wide variety of different kinds of leaves.

The shapes of leaves are even more varied than their colours. Some are flat and wide, some are narrow and needle-like, others thick and fleshy. Flowers come in all different shapes too. They range from enormous blooms, through elegant trumpet shapes to tiny, dainty flowerheads. The varied shapes of flowers and leaves help them survive in their chosen environment.

You will need

leaves and flowers	a paint brush
paper	a roller
thick paint	newspaper

gerbera

piggy-back plant

poplar

laurel

fern

a compound leaf

a lobed leaf

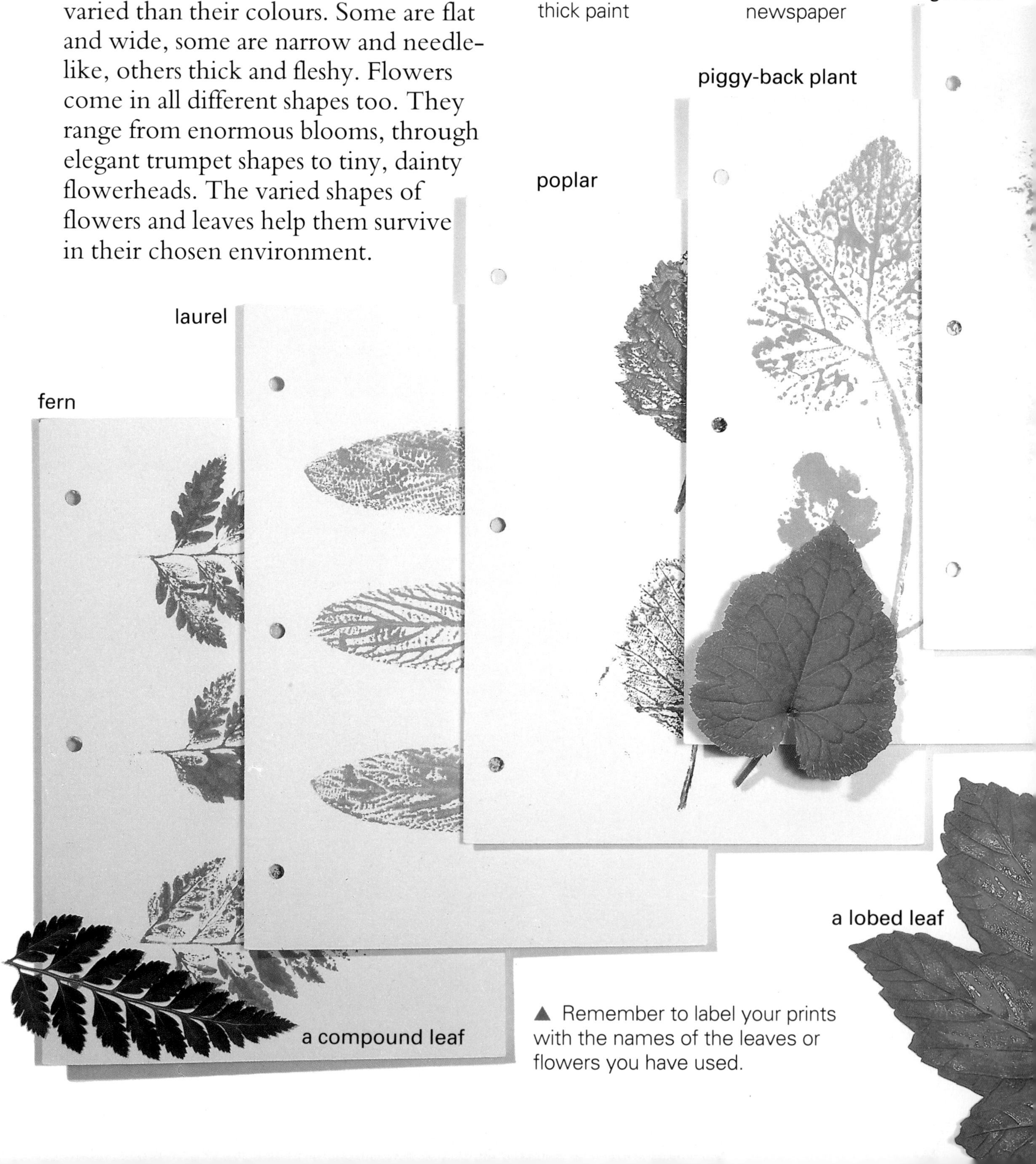

▲ Remember to label your prints with the names of the leaves or flowers you have used.

daisy

MAKE it WORK!

Make a collection of prints of all sorts of leaves and flowers. Can you think of any reasons why any of them may have a particular shape?

1 Use a large paint brush to cover the underside of a leaf with a thin layer of paint.

2 Place the leaf paint-side down on the paper and cover with newspaper or brown paper.

3 Gently move the roller over the brown paper, pressing the paint onto the paper beneath.

4 To take prints from flower heads, just coat them with paint and press them firmly down onto the paper with your hand.

Leaves are divided into three main groups: simple leaves which have just one blade; lobed leaves, which are shaped rather like a duck's webbed foot; and compound leaves which look like several leaves attached to one stalk.

Plants are an important source of food. We eat fruits, which are basically seed pods, and we eat many different parts of vegetable plants. Carrots and turnips are roots, broccoli is a flower, asparagus is a stem and spinach is leaves.

MAKE it WORK!

Take a close look at different fruits and vegetables. Look at the textures. Some are dense and dry, and others are juicy. Can you tell which part of the plant they come from? Study their shapes and textures by making a collection of fruit and vegetable prints.

You will need
fruit and vegetables
white paper
thick paint
a paint brush

1 Slice through the fruit or vegetable at its fattest point, either across (horizontally) or down (vertically) – whichever you think will make the most interesting impression.

2 Cover the slice of vegetable or fruit you are going to print with a thin layer of thick paint.

3 Press the painted slice down firmly on the paper. Try to press down evenly just once, to avoid making any smudges.

4 Leave your prints to dry, then label them and put them in a folder (see page 24). Never eat fruit and vegetables which have been painted.

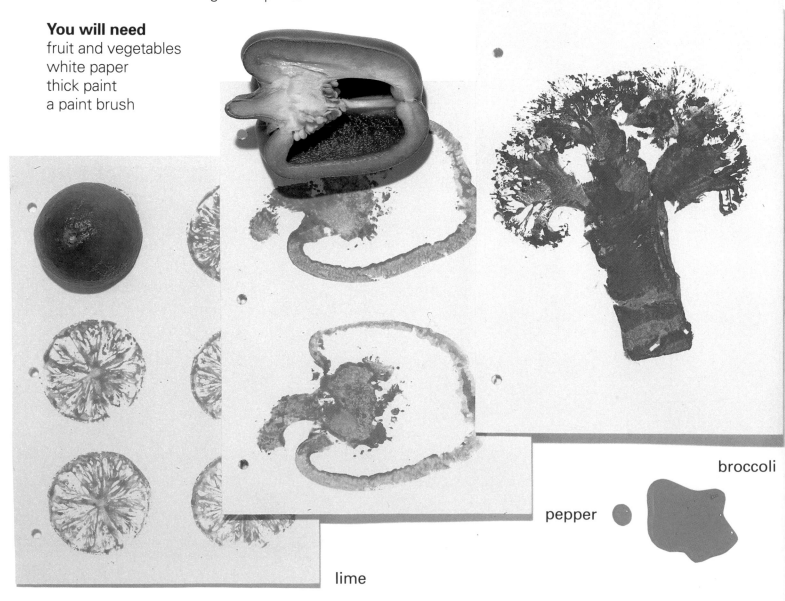

broccoli

pepper

lime

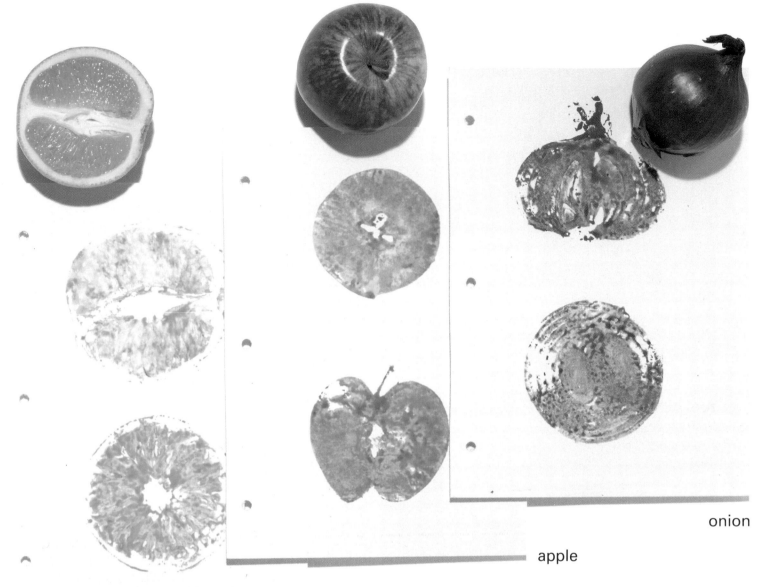

onion

apple

orange

Some animals eat only plants – they are called herbivores. Other animals just eat meat and are called carnivores. Some animals, and many humans, eat both plants and meat and are known as omnivores. However, plants are vital to the diet of every living thing. If there were no plants, herbivores would not have enough to eat and they would eventually die out. If there were no herbivores, the carnivores and omnivores would have no meat to eat either. So without plants, there would be no human or animal life on planet Earth at all.

FRUITS

If you look at flowers carefully, you will see that they all have the same four basic parts: the outer **sepals** which enclose the flower as it grows; the **corolla**, or petals; the **stamen,** small stalks that hold sacs of **pollen** grains; and the **carpels,** the parts where seeds grow.

You will need

card   thick coloured paper
flowers   waterproof glue
a craft knife   graph paper

MAKE it WORK!

Make some model flowers copied from real ones in a garden or in photographs.

2 On a piece of card, draw round the largest template and cut it out in one piece. Do the same for the other two templates. Glue the small one to the middle one and the middle one to the big one.

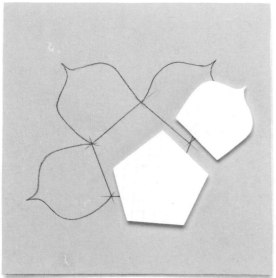

1 Draw a pentagon on a piece of graph paper, and then draw a petal shape with a base that fits onto one of the five sides of the pentagon. Repeat this process three times, each time making the pentagon a little smaller. Then cut out the shapes to make templates for your petals. You could also make a leaf template.

3 Cut and fold a piece of card to make stamens and carpels for your flower.

4 Fold up the petals of a flower so that it looks like an unopened bud. Then put it in a bowl of water and watch it blossom. You can dry out these flowers and use them again.

*Flowers are the **reproductive** part of the plant. They contain both the male cells, called the pollen, and the female cells, called the ovules or eggs. The ovules are inside the carpel. Reproduction takes place when pollen gets inside the carpel, and fertilizes an ovule.*

Most flowers are large and brightly coloured. The colours attract insects which feed on the sweet **nectar** inside the flower. Some flowers have patterns which cannot be seen by the human eye, but which are quite clear to insects.

MAKE it WORK!

Make a collection of flowers and then press them in a flower press. Make sure that you collect only common, cultivated flowers. You should never pick wild flowers.

You will need

two pieces of wood	four long screws
thick cardboard	four washers
blotting paper	four nuts

Ask an adult to help you cut the pieces of wood and drill holes in the four corners. Cut the pieces of cardboard and blotting paper the same size as the wood. Cut off the corners so that the screws do not go through them.

▶ Lay a piece of cardboard on the bottom piece of wood. Place a piece of blotting paper on top. Arrange a flower on this, then cover with a piece of blotting paper and a piece of cardboard. Repeat until the pile will just fit between the screws.

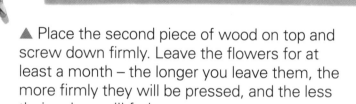

▲ Place the second piece of wood on top and screw down firmly. Leave the flowers for at least a month – the longer you leave them, the more firmly they will be pressed, and the less their colour will fade.

roses

purple heather

pink larkspur

Dried Flowers

Some flowers can be dried by hanging them upside down. Tie the flowers by the stalks and hang them from the ceiling. Some will take a week to dry out and others much longer. Some flowers lose their colour when they are dried. Experiment with different types of flowers to see which ones work best. You could try using leafy stems too.

Many plants need the help of insects to bring the ovules and pollen together to make a seed. Insects such as bees are attracted by the bright colours of the flowers and by the sweet nectar. A bee enters a flower for a drink of nectar and leaves carrying pollen. When it enters the next flower, the pollen is rubbed off the bee's body and onto the ovules of the new flower, so that the ovule is fertilized.

▲ Arrange your pressed flowers on thin card, and when you are happy with the position of the stem and leaves, stick them down with rubber solution glue. You could label your collection and display it in a special file.

As soon as the ovule inside a flower has been pollinated, seeds develop. The seed holder which protects the growing seeds becomes the fruit of the plant.

Some plants just drop their seeds nearby, but most try to spread their seeds as far afield as possible. Some plants, like the dandelion, have parachute-like fruits to carry seeds on the wind. Some spiky fruits, such as burrs, attach themselves to animals' fur. Other delicious fruits, such as berries, are eaten by animals. The seeds pass through their bodies as waste, to be deposited in some far-off hedgerow.

lemon

pips

stone

peach

walnut

nut

▲ Split open some fruits to see what their seeds are like. A nut is a seed too – its shell is called the hard fruit of a nut tree or plant.

◄ **Spore Prints**

Mushrooms and toadstools do not have seeds like other plants. Instead, they have **spores**. These spores are contained beneath the cup.

Take an open mushroom and cut off the stalk. Place the cap on a piece of white paper open side down. Leave overnight, then carefully lift off the mushroom. The spores will have fallen out of the mushroom cap, forming a print.

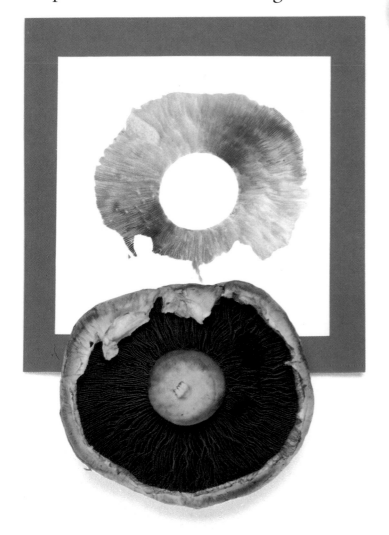

*Seeds do not begin to grow as soon as they reach the ground. They remain **dormant** until conditions are suitable for growth. In most cases they wait till spring arrives, but some seeds, such as those of desert plants, may lie dormant for years.*

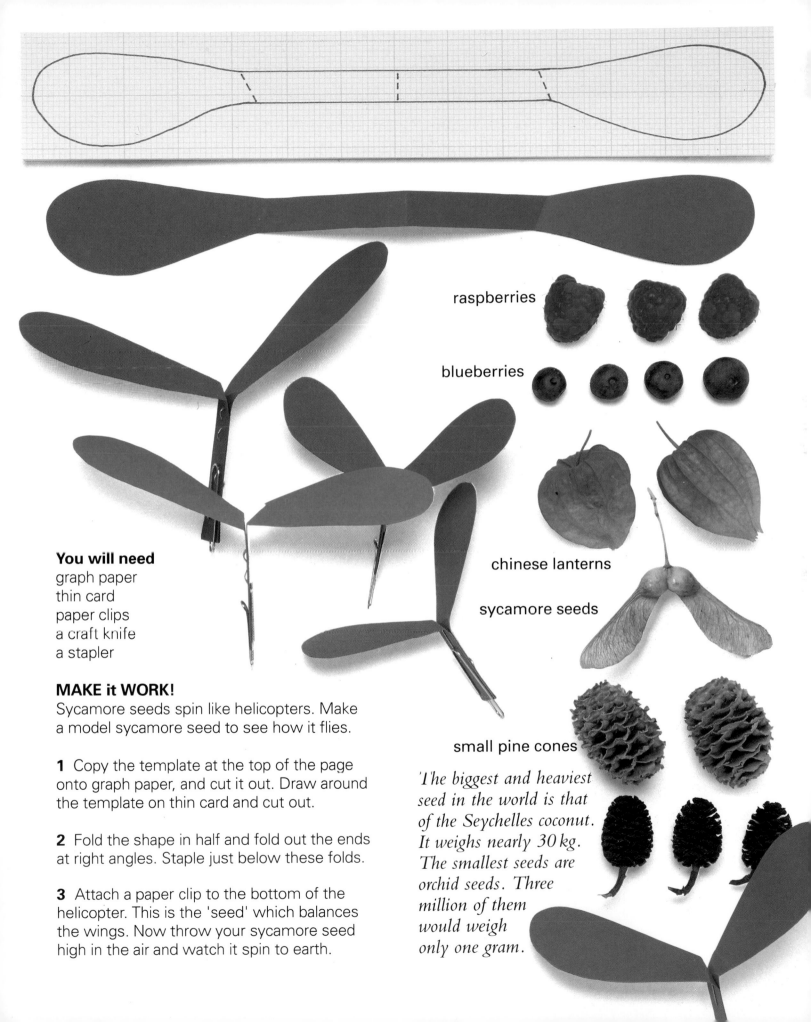

raspberries

blueberries

chinese lanterns

sycamore seeds

small pine cones

You will need
graph paper
thin card
paper clips
a craft knife
a stapler

MAKE it WORK!
Sycamore seeds spin like helicopters. Make a model sycamore seed to see how it flies.

1 Copy the template at the top of the page onto graph paper, and cut it out. Draw around the template on thin card and cut out.

2 Fold the shape in half and fold out the ends at right angles. Staple just below these folds.

3 Attach a paper clip to the bottom of the helicopter. This is the 'seed' which balances the wings. Now throw your sycamore seed high in the air and watch it spin to earth.

The biggest and heaviest seed in the world is that of the Seychelles coconut. It weighs nearly 30 kg. The smallest seeds are orchid seeds. Three million of them would weigh only one gram.

When plants die, they carry on being useful. Decaying plants return their nutrients to the soil, making it rich and fertile for the next generation. Plants begin to **decompose** as soon as they are picked. The mould spores that cause decay find their way into the plant as its protective layer of skin starts to break down, and they multiply very quickly. As food decays it shrivels and becomes lighter, because the mould spores are eating it up. Mould spores are **micro-organisms,** which means they are so small they can not be seen without a microscope.

You will need

fruit and vegetables	glue
a camera or coloured pencils	paper
brown manilla card	a craft knife

Be very careful with decayed food! Never taste it and wash your hands after touching it.

MAKE it WORK!

The best way to study decay is to watch it happen! Cut up some fruit and vegetables and leave them to decay. Try leaving pieces of food in different places to test the length of time they take to decay. Leave some on a warm window sill, some in a cool cupboard and some out of doors. Take photos of them every few days, or draw pictures of them, and keep a record of your findings in a special file box like the one on the right.

1 Attach your photos or drawings to cards. Cut out dividers to place between them.

orange

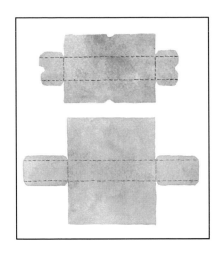

gluing and folding

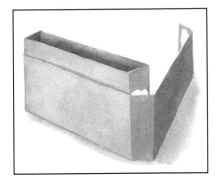

reinforcing the box

box and lid shapes

2 To make your file box, copy the shapes above onto smooth brown manilla card. Cut along the solid lines and score along the dotted ones. Fold along the scored lines and glue.

3 Glue an additional sleeve of card around the box, leaving a gap of about 3 cm at the top. This will help the lid to sit firmly on the box.

Bacteria are micro-organisms that cause diseases such as fevers and sore throats. There was no cure for such diseases until, in 1928, Alexander Fleming noticed mould growing on a laboratory dish of bacteria. The bacteria around the mould had been killed off by the same kind of mould that grows on cheese! This was the medicine penicillin, to which many people now owe their lives.

▼ The tabs on your dividers should be in different positions so you can read them easily.

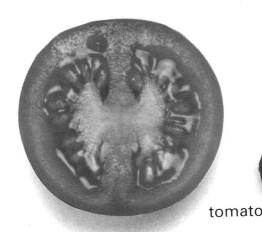

apple

tomato

Specimens all rot away in time unless they are preserved in some way. The only reason we know about the plants that grew on Earth millions of years ago is because many species were **fossilized**. The living plant fell into mud, leaving its mark in the soft earth. Fresh layers of mud trapped the plant, and the mud gradually hardened into rock, with the imprint of the plant still there, in vivid detail. Plant fossils, especially imprints of ferns and mosses, can be found in all kinds of rocks. A great many, especially tree roots, are found in underground mines.

▲ Can you make out the fossil of a plant inside this lump of coal?

1

2

MAKE it WORK!

You can make your own 'fossil', a permanent record of even your most delicate specimen, using soft modelling clay and plaster of Paris. A 3-D model will allow you to examine the shape and texture of your specimens long after the actual object has decayed.

1 Roll out a ball of modelling clay so that it is flat and smooth. Place the specimen on the clay and press it down with your fingers or the roller.

2 Carefully pull the specimen away from the modelling clay.

You will need
plaster of Paris
modelling clay
a roller
card
paper clips
plant specimen

Do you know what coal is made of? It is the result of millions of years of rotting plants and trees that sank into the earth and were later buried by more earth. The weight of these upper layers gradually squeezed all the moisture out of the rotting vegetation and pressed it into a solid mass of peat. The peat eventually hardened and became coal. Sometimes you can look at a piece of coal and see fossils of the original seed pods and roots. All the energy that was in those plants so long ago has turned into a substance called **carbon** *that still gives us energy today.*

▶ You could display your plaster casts in a shallow-sided box filled with clean sawdust to stop them getting knocked or chipped. You could also paint the plaster casts to show the colours of the original specimens.

3

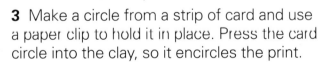

4

5

3 Make a circle from a strip of card and use a paper clip to hold it in place. Press the card circle into the clay, so it encircles the print.

4 Prepare a small amount of plaster of Paris and pour it into the card ring.

5 Leave the mould undisturbed overnight so that the plaster hardens properly. Then remove the clay and the card ring.

4

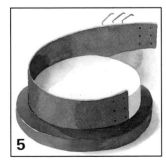

5

Have you noticed that if you spill beetroot on a white T-shirt, it doesn't wash out? The beetroot, like a number of other plants, is a natural dye. Today, most clothes are dyed with chemical dyes, but before these were invented, people had been using plants to bring colour into their lives for centuries.

MAKE it WORK!

Try extracting dye from onion skins and use it to dye a square of cotton or a T-shirt.

1 Peel the skin gently from a large brown onion, put the skins into a square of muslin, tie it up and put the bag into a pan of cold water.

2 Wet the fabric and put it in the pan. Bring the water to a gentle simmer, and keep it simmering until the fabric is the colour you want. It will take from twenty minutes to three hours. Stir regularly.

3 Lift the fabric out of the pan with the spoon and rinse in clean warm water until no more colour runs out. Allow to dry naturally.

You will need
For dyeing the fabric
a large saucepan
onion skins
muslin
a wooden spoon
For tie-dyeing
marbles and pebbles
white butcher's string
For keeping the dye
tea strainer
glass jars

Be careful!
Pans of boiling water are dangerous. Make sure your pan is big enough to hold the fabric without spilling. Never try to boil water without an adult to help you.

Tie-dyeing

The principle behind tie-dyeing is simply to stop the dye getting at certain parts of the fabric in order to make interesting patterns.

1 For a fairly free, random effect, just tie a knot in the centre of the fabric. The looser the knot the greater the spread of the dye. You can tie just one knot, or a series of knots.

2 For a striped pattern, roll the fabric into a loose sausage and tie string tightly around it at regular intervals if you want regular stripes, or with varying spaces if you want something more random.

3 For a circle pattern, put a pebble or marble in the centre, fold the cloth round it and secure with string. You can use a series of marbles of the same size or you can vary the pattern by using an assortment of pebbles.

Keeping the dye

You can use your dye again and again, as long as you keep it free from bits of vegetable matter which would soon start to rot. Even though you have tied up your plants, roots or skins securely in a muslin bag, little particles will inevitably escape. When the dye has cooled, remove the muslin bag, and pour the dye through a tea strainer into clean glass jars with screw-top lids. Label the jars and keep them in a dark cupboard, as exposure to sunlight will cause the colour to fade. As soon as they start to look cloudy, throw them out.

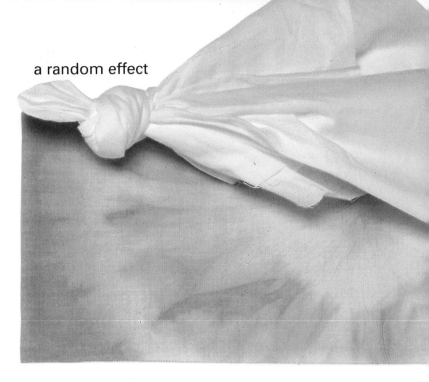

a random effect

a striped pattern

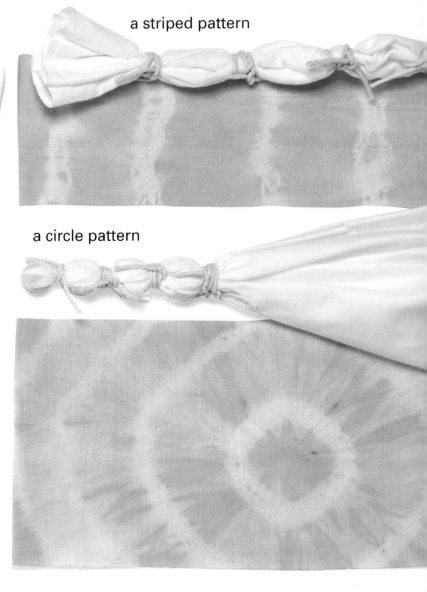

a circle pattern

Experiment with colour

Now you know how to extract dyes, try using different plants, roots and leaves. Some work very well and others not so well. You will also notice that results differ depending on which fabric you use. Cotton will come out paler than wool, because cotton absorbs less dye.

Some natural dyes are not colourfast, and will gradually wash out of the fabric if a substance called a fixer is not added. The fixer combines with the dye to make the colour enter the fibres of the fabric and produce a colour that will not fade.

▶ All the plants shown here will produce dyes that are naturally colourfast. Follow the directions on the previous page, remembering to put the plant, root, skins or powder into a muslin bag. For the turmeric powder (it's a spice used in Indian cooking) you may need a double layer of muslin. Notice that the colour of the fabrics dyed with the yellow flowers of the golden rod are in fact more brown than yellow.

In times gone by, among the most popular dyes were the intense yellow obtained from the stamens of the saffron crocus, the dark blue that comes from the Indian indigo plant (which we know better as the colour of blue jeans), and the orange-red of the henna plant which is used today as a hair dye.

The Ancient Phoenecians discovered that certain sea-snail shells, when crushed, produce a beautiful purple. It was a very costly dye, and only rich noblemen could afford to wear purple cloth. Particularly under the Romans, the colour became associated with wealth and power, and, to this day, kings and queens wear ceremonial robes of deep purple.

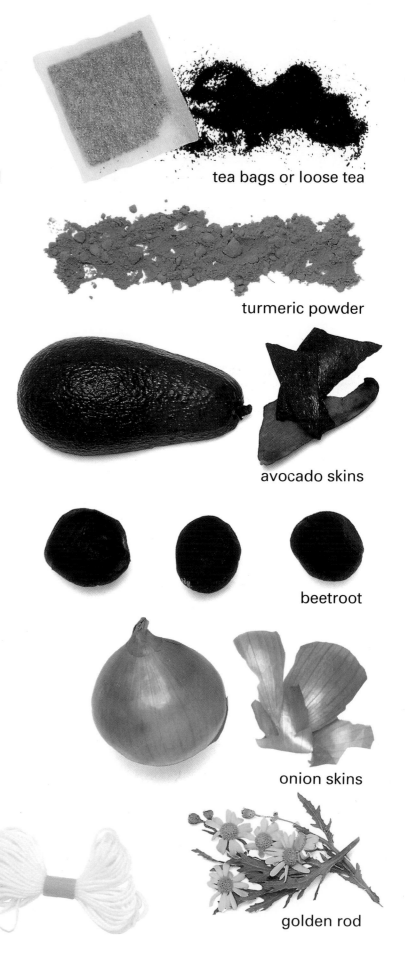

tea bags or loose tea

turmeric powder

avocado skins

beetroot

onion skins

golden rod

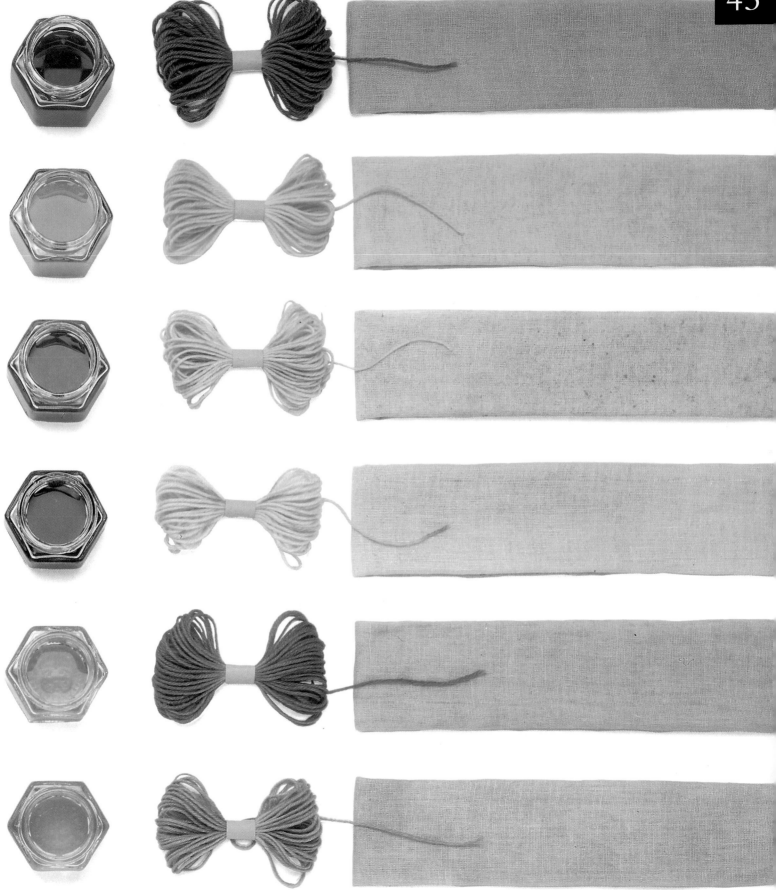

Algae Simple plants that live in water or damp places. Some algae are so small that you can not see the individual plants, but together they look like slime. Other algae, seaweed for example, are much larger.

Bacteria Microscopic plants. Many bacteria cause disease.

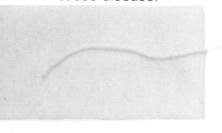

Calibrated If a stick is calibrated, it is marked out so that it can be used for measuring. A ruler is a calibrated piece of wood or plastic.

Carbon A substance that exists in many different forms and is found in all plants. Coal is a kind of carbon, made from the decomposed remains of plants and animals that died millions of years ago.

Carbon dioxide A colourless gas with no smell. It is an important part of the air that we breathe.

Carpels The female parts of flowers where the seeds are produced. Carpels contain the egg cells and a sticky area that catches pollen.

Cataloguing Cataloguing is the careful organizing, listing and storage of information, so that it can be found again easily.

Chlorophyll A chemical found in the stems and leaves of plants, which gives them their green colour. It takes in energy from the sun and helps to convert it into food for the plant.

Conifers Plants that grow their seeds in cones, such as fir trees, pines and cedars.

Corolla The rings of petals that form a flower.

Data Information that has been gathered in an organized way.

Deciduous Deciduous plants lose their leaves once a year, in the autumn.

Decompose To decay or rot. Dead plants decompose with the help of bacteria.

Dormant Inactive or asleep. When plants are dormant, they are not growing.

Environment The conditions that surround a plant or animal. Every living thing needs a particular environment (for instance, the right kind of soil, food and climate) to survive.

Evaporate When a liquid evaporates, it changes into a gas. For example, when water evaporates, it becomes steam or water vapour.

Ferns Plants which grow in moist, wooded areas. They have fronds rather than leaves.

Fossil Fossils are stones containing the imprint or remains of a plant or animal that lived in prehistoric times.

Fungi Fungi are plants that have no flower and do not contain the chemical chlorophyll. The commonest fungi are mushrooms and toadstools.

Hormones Hormones are chemicals found in every living thing. They are what make plants and animals grow.

Lichens Lichens are simple plants that grow in clumps like moss. Unlike most plants, they do not need soil, but can grow on rocks or the barks of trees.

Micro-organisms Plants or animals that are too small to be seen by the human eye. Bacteria are micro-organisms.

Mosses Tiny, simple plants that reproduce from spores rather than seeds. Moss grows in large clusters in damp, dark places.

Photosynthesis Photosynthesis is the process by which plants use sunlight to change water and carbon dioxide into food.

Pollen A powdery substance, which contains the male cells needed for a plant to reproduce.

Reproduction Making new life. Humans reproduce by having babies. In many plants, reproduction happens when male and female cells join together to make seeds.

Sap A sugary liquid that plants make to feed themselves. Sap is made from sunlight, water and air by the process of photosynthesis.

Scientist Someone who studies the world in a systematic way, to try and understand how it works.

Sepal The outer part of a flower bud. It protects the petals inside the bud as they grow.

Species A group of animals which appear to be the same and behave in a similar way.

Specimen A sample of a plant or animal. Scientists use specimens for observation and experiments.

Spores Spores are single plant cells, that are neither male nor female. Simple, non-flowering plants such as fungi and mosses reproduce from spores.

Stamen The male part of a flower. It consists of a stalk topped with two pollen sacs.

Theory An idea which tries to explain something. Scientific theories usually have to be proved by experiments before they are said to be true.